Sojourner Truth

by Helen Frost

Consulting Editor: Gail Saunders-Smith, Ph.D.

Consultant: Horace Porter, Chair,
African American World Studies Department,
University of Iowa

Pebble Books

an imprint of Capstone Press
Mankato, Minnesota

Pebble Books are published by Capstone Press
151 Good Counsel Drive, P.O. Box 669, Mankato, Minnesota 56002
http://www.capstone-press.com

1 2 3 4 5 6 08 07 06 05 04 03

Library of Congress Cataloging-in-Publication Data
Frost, Helen, 1949–
    Sojourner Truth / by Helen Frost.
    p. cm. —(Famous Americans)
    Summary: A simple biography of the former slave who spent most of her adult
life as a speaker against slavery and supporter of women's rights.
    Includes bibliographical references and index.
    ISBN 0-7368-1640-2 (hardcover)
    1. Truth, Sojourner, d. 1883—Juvenile literature. 2. African American
abolitionists—Biography—Juvenile literature. 3. African American women—
Biography—Juvenile literature. 4. Abolitionists—United States—Biography—
Juvenile literature. 5. Social reformers—United States—Biography—Juvenile
literature. [1. Truth, Sojourner, d. 1883. 2. Abolitionists. 3. Reformers. 4. African
Americans—Biography. 5. Women—Biography.] I. Title. II. Series.
E185.97.T8F76 2003
305.5'67'092—dc21   2002012278

Note to Parents and Teachers

The Famous Americans series supports national history standards
for units on people and culture. This book describes and illustrates
the life of Sojourner Truth. The photographs support early readers
in understanding the text. This book also introduces early readers to
subject-specific vocabulary words, which are defined in the Words
to Know section. Early readers may need assistance to read some
words and to use the Table of Contents, Words to Know, Read
More, Internet Sites, and Index/Word List sections of the book.

Table of Contents

Sojourner Truth was born in New York around 1797. Her name at birth was Isabella. She did not have a last name because she was a slave.

Sojourner being sold with six sheep

A slave's life was hard. Even young children worked hard as slaves. Isabella had to pick cotton and spin wool. She was sold to different owners three times.

a young slave being sold at an auction

Isabella grew up tall and strong. She later married a man named Thomas. They had five children.

a slave wedding celebration

10

Many people believed
that slavery was wrong.
In 1817, New York passed
a law to free some slaves.
In 1827, Isabella
became free.

Isabella's son Peter was five years old when he was sold to a slave owner. This sale was against the law in New York. Isabella went to court to win Peter back.

a New York courtroom in the mid-1800s

Isabella won her case.

Peter came home.

Isabella became the first African American woman to win a court case against a white man.

FREE LECTURE!

SOJOURNER TRUTH,

In 1843, Isabella changed her name to Sojourner Truth. A sojourner is a traveler. Sojourner traveled and spoke against slavery. Slavery was still legal in some states.

18

Sojourner had a strong, deep voice. People listened to her. She said that all slaves should be free. She said that women should have the same rights as men.

20

Sojourner lived to be very old. She died in 1883. People remember that she spoke the truth. Sojourner Truth helped change laws that were not fair.

Words to Know

African American—a person in the United States with an African background

court—a place where legal cases are heard and decided

free—able to do what you choose to do; after slaves became free, they could make their own decisions about work, marriage, and travel.

law—a rule made by the government that must be obeyed

legal—allowed by the law

right—something the law says that you can have or do

slave—a person owned by another person; slaves are not free to choose their work or their jobs.

truth—real facts

Read More

Leebrick, Kristal. *Sojourner Truth.* Let Freedom Ring. Mankato, Minn.: Bridgestone Books, 2002.

McLoone, Margo. *Sojourner Truth.* Photo-Illustrated Biographies. Mankato, Minn.: Bridgestone Books, 1997.

Spinale, Laura. *Sojourner Truth.* Journey to Freedom. Chanhassen, Minn.: Child's World, 2000.

Internet Sites

Track down many sites about Sojourner Truth. Visit the FACT HOUND at *http://www.facthound.com*

IT IS EASY! IT IS FUN!

1) Go to *http://www.facthound.com*

2) Type in: 0736816402

3) Click on "FETCH IT" and FACT HOUND will find several links hand-picked by our editors.

Relax and let our pal FACT HOUND do the research for you!

Index/Word List

African
  American, 15
born, 5
case, 15
children, 7, 9
court, 13, 15
died, 21
fair, 21
free, 11, 19
law, 11, 13, 21
legal, 17
man, 9, 15, 19
married, 9

name, 5, 17
New York, 5, 11,
  13
owners, 7, 13
passed, 11
Peter, 13
rights, 19
sale, 13
slave, 5, 7, 11,
  13, 19
slavery, 17
sold, 7, 13
son, 13

spoke, 17, 21
states, 17
strong, 9, 19
tall, 9
Thomas, 9
traveler, 17
truth, 21
voice, 19
white, 15
win, 15
worked, 7

Word Count: 232
Early-Intervention Level: 18

Editorial Credits
Hollie J. Endres, editor; Clay Schotzko/Icon Productions, cover designer;
   Molly Nei, designer; Karrey Tweten, photo researcher

Photo Credits
Corbis/Bettman, cover, 1, 12
Ed Wong-Ligda, 4
Getty Images/Hulton Archive, 6, 18; Millbrook Press, 8
Peggy Michael, 14
PictureQuest, 20
State Archives of Michigan, 10, 16

The author thanks the children's library staff at the Allen County Public Library
in Fort Wayne, Indiana, for research assistance.